# HURRICANES AND TYPHOONS

© Aladdin Books Ltd 2005

New edition published in the
United States in 2005 by:
Stargazer Books
c/o The Creative Company
123 South Broad Street
P.O. Box 227
Mankato, Minnesota 56002

Designer: Stephen Woosnam-Savage
Editors: Fiona Robertson
         Libby Volke
Picture Research: Emma Krikler
                  Brian Hunter Smart
Illustrator: Guy Smith

Printed in UAE

Library of Congress Cataloging-in-Publication Data

Dineen, Jacqueline.
   Hurricanes and typhoons / by Jacqueline Dineen.
      p. cm.-- (Natural disasters)
   Includes index.
   ISBN 1-932799-06-0 (alk. paper)
      1. Storms--Juvenile literature. 2. Hurricanes--Juvenile literature.
      3. Typhoons--Juvenile literature. I. Title. II. Series.

QC941.3.D56 2004
551.55'2--dc22
                                              2004040809

# *Natural Disasters*

# HURRICANES AND TYPHOONS

## JACQUELINE DINEEN

STARGAZER BOOKS

# CONTENTS

# INTRODUCTION

Hurricanes, typhoons, and cyclones are the names given to massive tropical storms in different parts of the world. Tropical storms differ from ordinary storms in several important ways. For example, the winds in a tropical storm are always rotational. They whirl around in a circular motion at speeds far greater than those in any ordinary storm. In addition, while the energy unleashed by an ordinary storm is sufficient to provide the whole of the USA with power for twenty minutes, the energy unleashed by a tropical storm is 12,000 times as powerful. Such terrible power has brought death and destruction to many areas of the world, as was shown by the cyclone that battered Bangladesh in April 1991, killing over 250,000 people.

# THE WORLD'S WINDS

Winds are caused by movement of warm and cold air. Warm air is lighter than cold air and so rises, creating an area of low pressure at the earth's surface. In other places, cold air sinks down toward the earth's surface, and spreads out to create an area of high pressure. Winds are therefore movements of air over the earth's surface from areas of high pressure to areas of low pressure.

At the equator, where the sun's rays are strongest, warm air is constantly rising, which leads to areas of low pressure. At the poles, the sun's rays are weaker. Air is cooled over the icy polar caps and sinks to create areas of high pressure. Around the earth, movements of air between areas of high and low pressure result in convection cells (right).

The winds are complicated by the spinning of the earth, which bends the flows of air clockwise in the Northern Hemisphere, and counterclockwise in the Southern Hemisphere. This is known as the "Coriolis effect."

↓ This map shows the prevailing global winds and the breeding grounds in which tropical storms can develop (shaded areas).

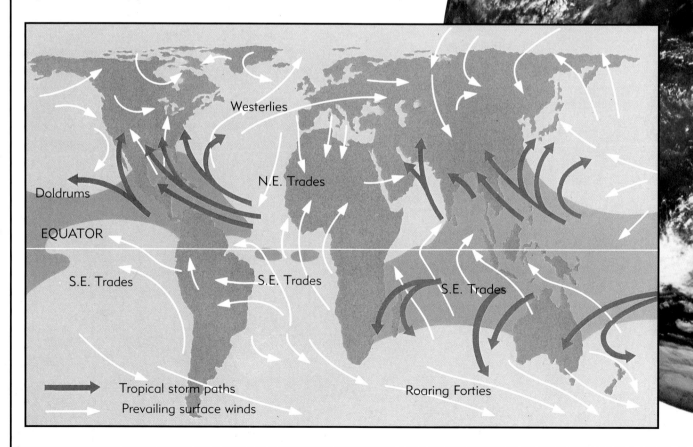

Westerlies

Doldrums

EQUATOR

N.E. Trades

S.E. Trades

S.E. Trades

S.E. Trades

→ Tropical storm paths

→ Prevailing surface winds

Roaring Forties

## Wind cells

The heating effect of the sun on the earth's surface results in three massive "cells" of rising and falling air. At the earth's surface, winds blowing from high pressure to low pressure areas are bent by the Coriolis effect.

↑ Satellite pictures show the main cloud formations over the earth.

## Clouds

Clouds are formed when air cools to a temperature at which it can no longer hold all its water as vapor. Water droplets form, which appear as clouds. Different types of clouds are shown below. Heavy, black cumulonimbus clouds often warn of a storm.

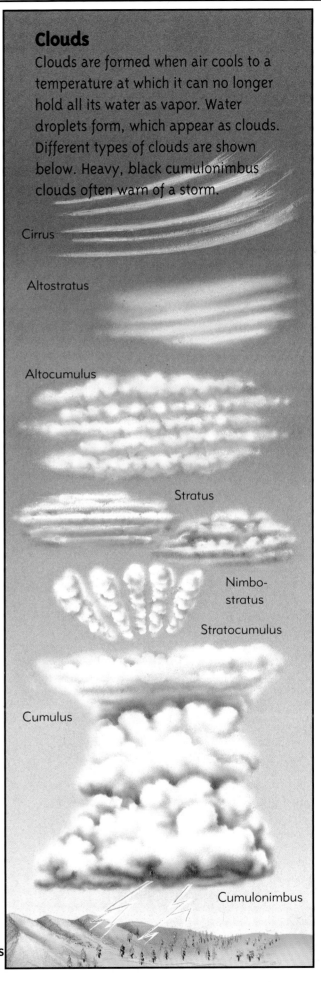

Cirrus

Altostratus

Altocumulus

Stratus

Nimbo-stratus

Stratocumulus

Cumulus

Cumulonimbus

# WHAT IS A HURRICANE?

When cyclonic winds reach speeds of more than 40 mph, they are officially "tropical storms," and are assigned a name. If the winds exceed speeds of 75 mph on the Beaufort Wind Scale then they are redefined as hurricanes, typhoons, or cyclones, depending on their location. They are called "hurricanes" when they occur over the Atlantic Ocean, "typhoons" in the Far East, and "cyclones" in the Indian Ocean.

A hurricane is a large spinning wind system that develops over warm seas near the equator, in areas known as the tropics.

The tropics are the hottest parts of the world, and experience the most extreme weather conditions. Air heated by the sun rises very swiftly, which creates areas of very low pressure. As the warm air rises, it becomes loaded with moisture that condenses into massive thunderclouds. Cool air rushes in to fill the space that is left, but because of the constant turning of the earth on its axis, the air is bent inward, and then spirals upward with great force. The swirling winds rotate faster and faster, forming a huge circle that can be up to 1,200 miles across.

↑ In summer 2001, two typhoons (Durian and Utor) raged across the South China Sea in the space of a week. The Philippines were badly affected.

→ The shattered remains of Darwin in Australia after Cyclone Tracy hit the area on Christmas Day in 1974. Tracy's winds reached 150 mph and battered the city for over four hours. 48,000 inhabitants were evacuated and 8,000 homes destroyed.

## Extreme conditions

A spectacular part of tropical storms are the long, low thunderclouds that can be seen rolling across this landscape. The tinges of gray-black at the edges of the clouds are the result of the undercurrents of cold air that force the moisture in the warmer air above to condense very quickly. It is these clouds that bring the torrential downpours of rain that accompany most thunderstorms. Thunder and lightning may also occur.

# A HURRICANE BEGINS

Hurricanes usually begin in the steamy late summer in the tropics when the seas are at their warmest. For a hurricane to develop, the sea surface must have a temperature of at least 79 degrees Fahrenheit. When warm air rises from the seas and condenses into clouds, massive amounts of heat are released. The result of this mixture of heat and moisture is often a collection of thunderstorms, from which a tropical storm can develop.

The trigger for most Atlantic hurricanes is an easterly wave, a band of low pressure moving westward (see illustration), which may have begun as an African thunderstorm.

Vigorous thunderstorms and high winds combine to create a cluster of thunderstorms that can become the seedling for a tropical storm.

Typhoons in the Far East and cyclones in the Indian Ocean often develop from a thunderstorm in the equatorial trough (see below). During the hurricane season, the Coriolis effect of the earth's rotation starts the winds in the thunderstorm spinning in a circular motion.

At the center of the storm is a calm, cloudless area called the "eye," where there is no rain, and the winds are fairly light.

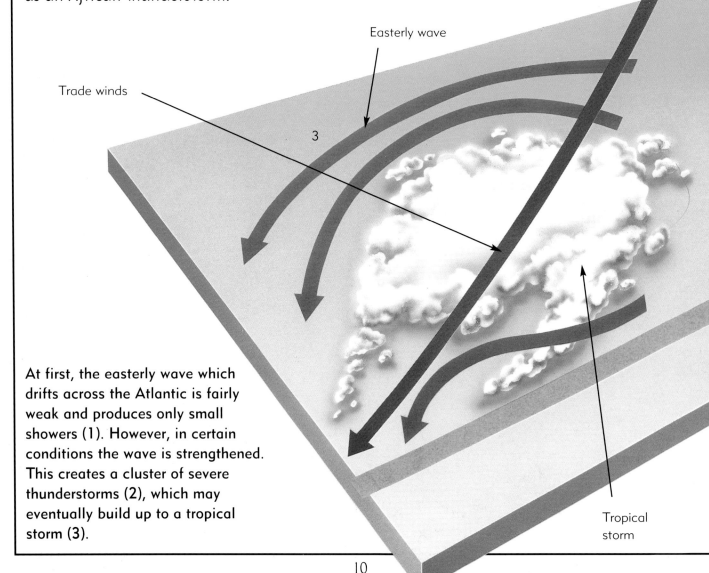

Easterly wave

Trade winds

3

At first, the easterly wave which drifts across the Atlantic is fairly weak and produces only small showers (1). However, in certain conditions the wave is strengthened. This creates a cluster of severe thunderstorms (2), which may eventually build up to a tropical storm (3).

Tropical storm

## Hurricane detection

The National Hurricane Center was formed in 1959 in the United States. One of its aims is to investigate the amount of energy in a hurricane, and to understand how the energy is distributed. Other objectives include studying how hurricanes work, and in what ways their impact could be controlled and reduced. Research is also being carried out concerning the forces that make hurricanes move from where they first begin.

Shown here, a hurricane researcher is collecting and analyzing data that helps identify potential hurricanes.

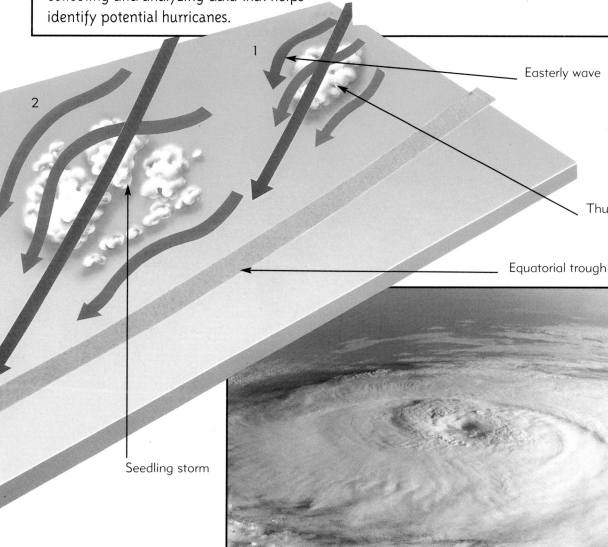

1

2

Easterly wave

Thunderstorm

Equatorial trough

Seedling storm

➤ An Atlantic hurricane photographed from space. The calm, cloudless region of the eye, with the fury of the hurricane raging all around it, is clearly visible.

# THE BUILD-UP

As the hurricane builds up, it begins to move. It is sustained by a steady flow of warm, moist air. The strongest winds and heaviest rains are found in the towering clouds that merge into a wall about 12-18 miles from the storm's center. Winds around the eye can reach speeds of up to 120 mph, and a fully developed hurricane pumps out about two million tons of air per second. This results in more rain being released in a day than falls in a year on a city like New York.

The hurricane travels at speeds of between 9 and 31 mph. When it hits an area of cold sea or land, it enters a cold, inhospitable climate, where its supply of moist air is cut off. The eye quickly disappears and the storm begins to die.

However, it is when it hits the land that a hurricane, typhoon, or cyclone causes most damage. Ninety percent of victims are claimed when the storm first smashes ashore, bringing with it not only powerful winds, but huge waves called "storm surges."

Clouds
The clouds are kept swirling around the eye by the strength of the wind. They spin around like a huge pinwheel.

← The air in the eye is calm and smooth at most heights, and is much warmer than that of the surrounding clouds of the hurricane.

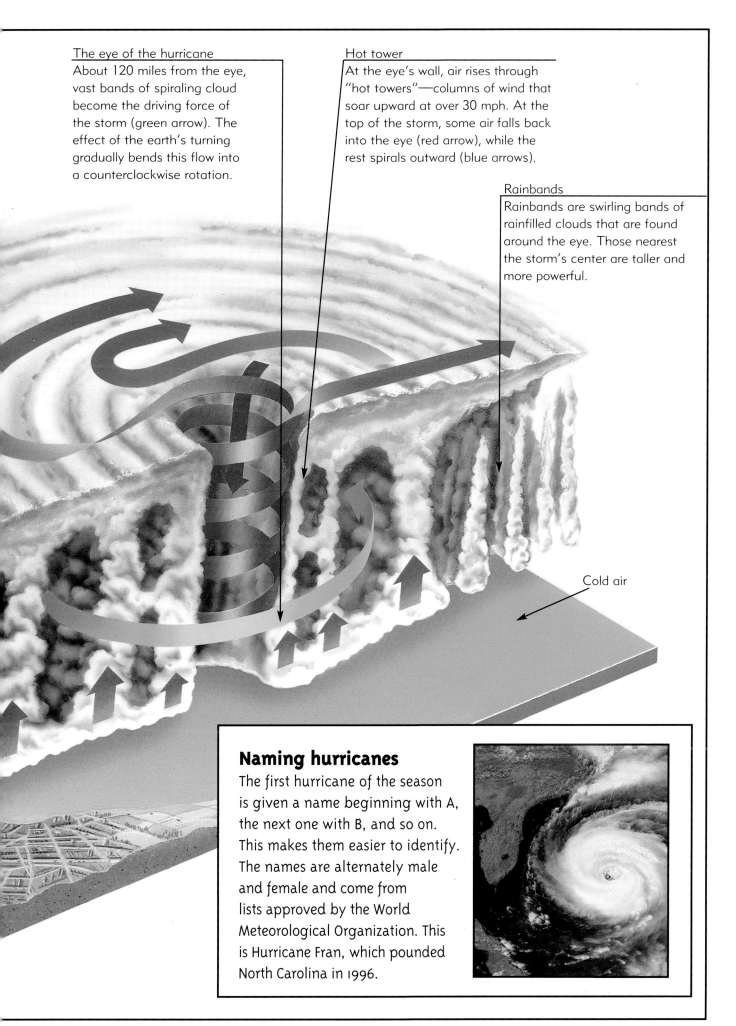

**The eye of the hurricane**
About 120 miles from the eye, vast bands of spiraling cloud become the driving force of the storm (green arrow). The effect of the earth's turning gradually bends this flow into a counterclockwise rotation.

**Hot tower**
At the eye's wall, air rises through "hot towers"—columns of wind that soar upward at over 30 mph. At the top of the storm, some air falls back into the eye (red arrow), while the rest spirals outward (blue arrows).

**Rainbands**
Rainbands are swirling bands of rainfilled clouds that are found around the eye. Those nearest the storm's center are taller and more powerful.

Cold air

## Naming hurricanes
The first hurricane of the season is given a name beginning with A, the next one with B, and so on. This makes them easier to identify. The names are alternately male and female and come from lists approved by the World Meteorological Organization. This is Hurricane Fran, which pounded North Carolina in 1996.

# THE STORM SURGE

The deadly companion of every tropical storm is the storm surge—the huge mounds of seawater that are whipped up by the powerful winds.

The first sign of a storm surge can occur nearly a week before the actual hurricane, typhoon, or cyclone. Winds move outward much faster than the storm itself and whip up the sea into waves up to 5 ft high along the coastline. When the storm is about 100 miles from land, huge waves driven by its winds begin to crash ashore. The deafening roar of the waves' surf can be heard for miles inland. This is followed by the most deadly and destructive element of the surge, as the bulge of water that forms beneath the storm's eye smashes ashore.

The effects of such storm surges are far-reaching. Low-lying coastal areas can be devastated by the severe floods that result, and many lives and homes may be lost. In the Far East, typhoons build up in the western Pacific Ocean and batter Japan and the Asian mainland. Cyclones that begin in the Indian Ocean can veer south toward East Africa.

## Storm surges

A storm surge builds up out at sea as a tropical storm races in toward the shore. The sea level rises above the height of protective sand dunes on the shore. As the sea rushes in, it flattens the dunes and swamps the land behind them. This town will be flooded by the storm surge.

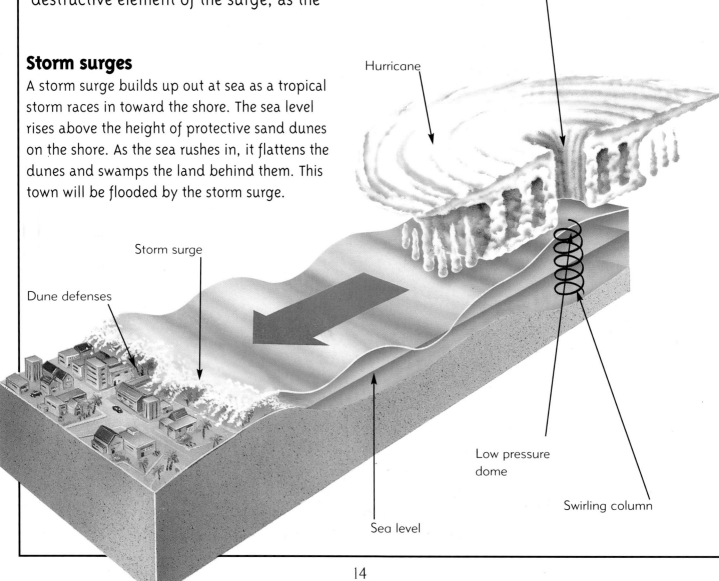

Hurricane's eye

Hurricane

Storm surge

Dune defenses

Low pressure dome

Sea level

Swirling column

## Into the storm

The unpredictability of tropical storms and the speed at which they can suddenly change course have caught the crew of many ships at sea unawares. Equipped to deal with such emergencies are tug boats like the "Abeille-Languedoc" (shown right), which often have to undertake rescue missions arising from storms at sea.

## Sea storms in history

For ships at sea, no storm poses a greater threat than a fully-developed hurricane or winds of hurricane force. Although sailing ships were built to withstand gales and storms, the winds and mountainous seas created by such extreme weather phenomena often caused great damage. In this illustration, desperate sailors are seen trying to stay afloat as their ships sink in the maelstrom of the English Channel. This storm was one of the worst in England's history. It struck in November 1703, and its hurricane-force winds claimed about 8,000 lives and destroyed more than 14,000 homes.

↑ A U.S. destroyer caught in the enormous waves formed by a typhoon in December, 1944. The storm was so severe that the waves were described by the captain of the ship as being "like vertical mountains."

# A FREAK ON LAND

In many ways, a tornado resembles a miniature hurricane. However, tornadoes are far more powerful than hurricanes. This is because their fearsome energy is concentrated into a violently spinning column of air, less than a mile across.

Unlike hurricanes, tornadoes tend to form over land. Central North America experiences more tornadoes than anywhere else in the world. They usually occur during cloudy, stormy weather and descend from a severe thunderstorm as a rapidly-spinning white funnel of cloud. Dust and soil are drawn up into the funnel in a spiral that can be seen hurtling across the landscape. A screaming roar pierces the ears and scythe-like winds cut through even the strongest of buildings. Cars, mobile homes, and even airplanes have been picked up, carried away, and then dropped and smashed like toys.

When it touches the ground, the tornado quickly turns gray with dust and develops ragged edges. It becomes weaker, can no longer suck up the air in its path, and gradually dies out.

## The ultimate storm

Tornadoes are the strongest winds in the world and can often cause total destruction of the area they hit. As the tornado's funnel tightens, the winds begin to spin faster and faster. The rotating winds pick up dust and debris, and the tornado is surrounded by an envelope of dust. Inside the dust envelope, the strongest winds can be found rotating at speeds of up to 190 mph around a calm central eye of low pressure. This is known as the funnel cloud. Because the tornado's lowest pressure is near the ground, air that is sucked up into the funnel begins to gain speed as it spirals around the eye. The air gradually slows down and spreads out as it reaches the heavy cumulonimbus clouds that are found at the top of the tornado.

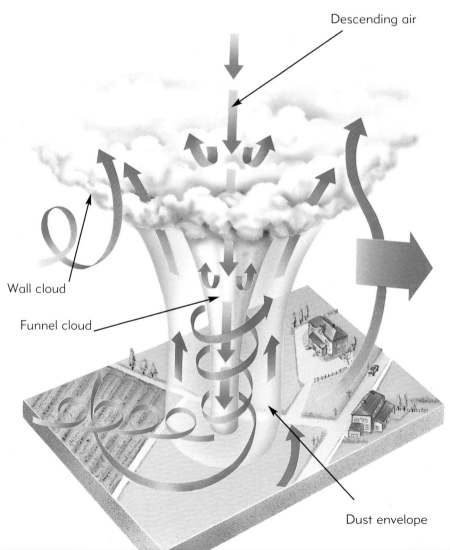

Descending air

Wall cloud

Funnel cloud

Dust envelope

A waterspout is a funnel of air that extends down from a cloud over the sea. In the same way as a tornado sucks up soil and debris, the waterspout sucks up great quantities of water. This gives the funnel its dark color (right). Water-spouts are much weaker than tornadoes and their winds rarely exceed 50 mph. They only last for about 15 minutes and occur mainly in shallow coastal waters.

# THE DAMAGE

For anyone caught in a hurricane, the experience is a terrifying one. Fierce, whirling winds rip across the countryside, overturning cars and heavy trucks. Trees are ripped from the ground by their roots, and whole buildings can be lifted from their foundations.

Some of the worst disasters occur near coastal areas, where stormy seas contribute to the havoc that is wreaked. In 1938, one of the most powerful hurricanes in history swept through Long Island, New York. In just seven hours, the storm killed at least 600 people and destroyed the homes of over 60,000. The total damage was estimated at the enormous sum of one third of a billion dollars. The storm destroyed 26,000 cars and 29,000 miles of electric, telegraph, and telephone cables, and flooded thousands of acres of land.

In 1998, Hurricane Mitch struck Central America and became the deadliest Atlantic hurricane since 1780. Winds of 180 mph tore up trees and blew the roofs off buildings. Torrential rain lashed down, causing massive flooding and landslides. Over 11,000 people lost their lives to Mitch.

↑ The storm surge that hit Bangladesh in 1991 claimed hundreds of thousands of lives.
← Coastal areas often feel a storm's full force. In 2001, tropical storm Allison hammered U.S. states along the Atlantic and Gulf Coasts.
↓ Mitch ruined transport networks across Central America. This Guatemalan road has been completely washed away.

# PLOTTING THE PATH

No one can do anything to prevent a hurricane. The only thing weather forecasters can do is to try and plot the hurricane's path. People living in the area can then be warned and evacuated if necessary.

Weather stations all over the world exchange information about winds, rainfall, cloud, temperature, and air pressure. Satellites in space circle the earth and take photographs of the atmosphere from above, which can be used to show how clouds are forming.

At the first signs that a tropical storm is building up, information can be fed into computers to try to predict its course. First, a band of low pressure may develop over tropical seas, in an area that has spawned tropical storms in the past. For example, storms near the west coast of Africa have led to violent hurricanes and storm surges, that later hit the islands of the Caribbean. In 1985, hurricane experts in the United States spotted a storm of this type and plotted its course as it developed into Hurricane Gloria. One million people had to be evacuated from their homes on the east coast of the United States.

↓ The colors on satellite pictures of tropical storms help meteorologists measure temperature and rainfall in different parts of the hurricane, and estimate the storm's strength and course.

→ Scientists at Colorado's Environmental Research Laboratories are combining sophisticated new instruments with computer technology to create a new "minute by minute" weather warning system. The system uses special radar devices, called profilers, that are directed toward the sky. Sophisticated computer equipment and other monitoring systems are also used. In this way, changes in the atmosphere can quickly be detected, and storms can be recognized even as they are forming. The storm's movement is then charted on screens (shown right).

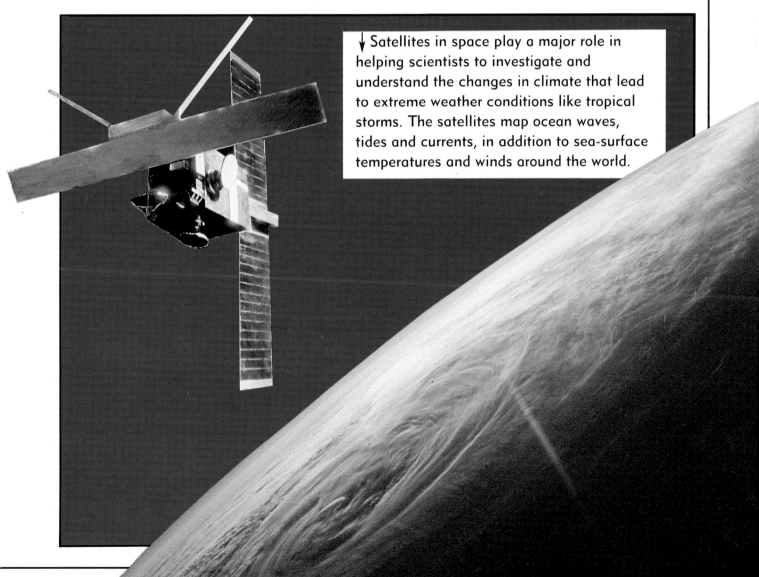

↓ Satellites in space play a major role in helping scientists to investigate and understand the changes in climate that lead to extreme weather conditions like tropical storms. The satellites map ocean waves, tides and currents, in addition to sea-surface temperatures and winds around the world.

# GETTING IT WRONG

The United States is often lashed by hurricanes, but the countries of Europe rarely find themselves in the path of such violent storms.

In the autumn of 1987, however, a freak storm with hurricane-force winds swept across the Atlantic from the United States. Although the storm was not a fully-developed hurricane with swirling, rotating winds, it nevertheless wreaked havoc in the countries it hit. The winds strengthened as they approached Europe. First Spain and Portugal were pounded by strong gales. Forecasters expected the winds to die down before they reached Britain, but their predictions were wrong. The winds became stronger still as they blew on toward northern France and southern England.

The full force of the storm struck in the middle of the night, as everyone slept. Had the storm arrived during the day, many more people would probably have been killed. As it was, the main damage was to buildings and trees. Thousands of trees were uprooted like matchsticks and thrown across roads and over cars and buildings. Many roads were blocked by the fallen debris. Roofs and chimneys were blown off and flying roof slates and tiles hurtled through the air. Some buildings collapsed, and millions of people were without power for several days because of damage to power supplies.

↑ Huge waves battered the coast of Normandy as the storm crossed northern France. For four days, rising tides spilled seawater over nearby farmland, destroying crops and livestock, and rendering the land useless for at least the next five years.

## The hurricanes that move inland

In 1954, Hurricane Hazel swept across the Caribbean Sea and intensified as it hit the east coast of the United States. The hurricane brought torrential rains and record winds to many areas, including Maryland, Virginia, and New York City. In Washington, government workers were allowed to go home early. Many had to cling to lamp posts for support against the high winds as they tried to cross the roads (shown below).

↓ The storm that battered Europe in 1987 caused millions of dollars worth of damage to property. In England, the south coast suffered the most storm damage.

# LIVING WITH THE THREAT

The threat of hurricanes is an ever-present one. Even if precautions are taken, they can still cause misery and devastation.

However, many of the world's developing countries do not have the resources to take precautions or build defenses. Unfortunately, it is often these areas that are hit most severely by tropical storms.

In June 1999, a cyclone with winds of 125 mph hammered the southeastern coast of Bangladesh, creating storm surges that left 800,000 people homeless.

India suffered the worst cyclone tragedy of recent years in 1999, when a supercyclone ripped into Orissa State, bringing storm waves 20 feet high, killing 10,000 people, and affecting two million people in total.

## Building defenses

Sea walls are the best protection for towns near the sea. Some walls curve outward at the top so that the waves are turned back on themselves as they break against them. Others have teeth or ridges that are designed to break up the waves and reduce their impact. When floods do occur, efficient pumping stations are needed to get rid of the water quickly. Shutters can be used to protect windows from smashing. The window in the picture below has been covered with strips of tape to stop it from shattering.

## Clearing up the mess

The damage caused by a hurricane can take months or even years to repair. People are often forced to salvage what little they have left from their flooded or wrecked homes (below right). Roads have to be cleared and fallen debris removed (below). Electricity and phone cables have to be repaired. Emergency food and water supplies may have to be brought into the affected area. Two million homes were destroyed or damaged in the Orissa supercyclone. When the storm finally died out after 36 relentless hours, many survivors faced days or weeks without water, food, or shelter.

# ARE WE CAUSING MORE?

Hurricanes are sustained by warm, moist air. The countries of northern Europe have a fairly cool climate. So why have they been hit by hurricanes in recent years?

One theory is that global warming is having some effect. As the planet heats up, more parts of the world are developing the kind of climate that is ideal for tropical storms.

The gases in the earth's atmosphere act like the glass of a greenhouse, trapping enough heat from the sun to keep the planet warm enough for life. This is known as the "Greenhouse Effect." One of the main greenhouse gases is carbon dioxide. Other greenhouse gases are methane, water vapor, and chlorofluorocarbons (CFCs). The only way we can prevent global warming is by controlling the amounts of these gases that are released into the atmosphere.

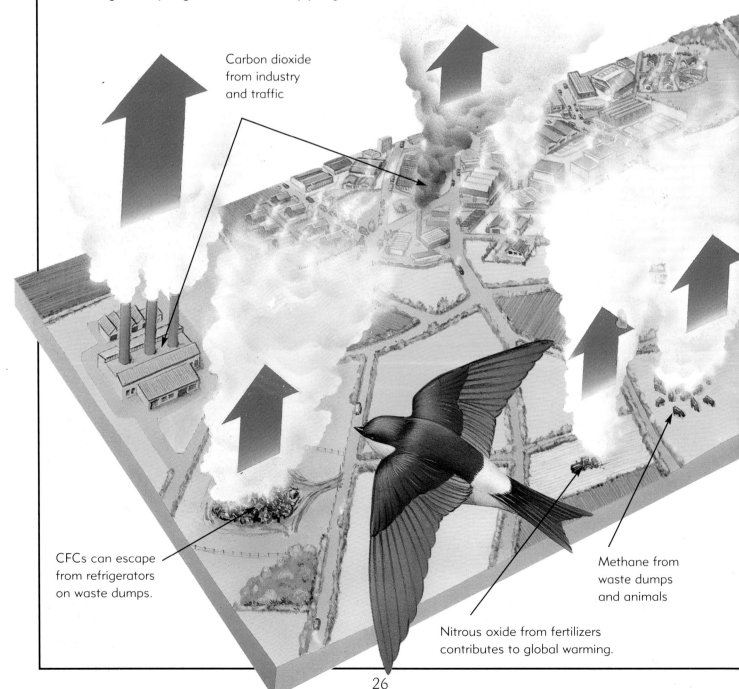

Carbon dioxide from industry and traffic

CFCs can escape from refrigerators on waste dumps.

Methane from waste dumps and animals

Nitrous oxide from fertilizers contributes to global warming.

## The Greenhouse Effect

The atmosphere allows sunlight through to heat the earth, but traps some of the heat that radiates back toward space. This is similar to the way the glass in a greenhouse works, and so it is called the Greenhouse Effect. The gases that prevent some of the heat from escaping into space are known as greenhouse gases. They help to maintain the right temperatures on earth for life. If too many greenhouse gases are present, however, too much warmth is trapped, causing global temperatures to rise.

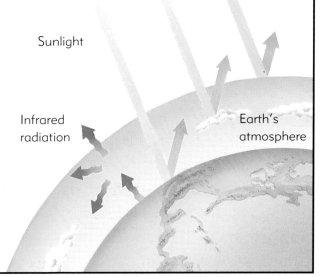

Sunlight

Infrared radiation

Earth's atmosphere

Water vapor

→ Carbon dioxide occurs naturally in the atmosphere, but it is also produced by burning fuels in factories and power plants, and is emitted in vehicle exhaust fumes. Plants absorb carbon dioxide, but clearing large areas of rainforests means that there are fewer plants to do this. Levels of carbon dioxide in the atmosphere therefore increase.

# WHAT CAN WE DO?

In developed, industrialized countries, meteorologists are working on ways of improving information and warning systems, and of pinpointing danger zones. However, even when sophisticated equipment is used, and information is processed by computer, hurricanes can still take people by surprise. If the storm suddenly changes course, the evacuation of an area may not be possible. Precautions should therefore be taken to reduce the impact of the hurricane, typhoon, or cyclone and to offer protection for people in its path.

In low-lying areas, special shelters can be built for this purpose. Bangladesh has 1,200 cyclone shelters—many of which were built after the 1991 tragedy. They are raised 13 feet from the ground and built to withstand great forces. Shelters can hold up to 1,500 people each, and are used as public buildings, such as schools, during the dry season.

## Preventing global warming

There are several ways to reduce the amount of harmful greenhouse gases currently being pumped into the atmosphere. For example, to reduce carbon dioxide levels, we must start by burning less fossil fuels, both in industry (below) and at home. This can be done by using alternative sources of energy, like wind, water, and solar power, that do not release carbon dioxide into the atmosphere. Homes and factories can be made more efficient so they use less energy, and forests can be replanted to stop carbon dioxide building up in the atmosphere.

→ Teams of experts worldwide gather information on weather changes. Once a storm is identified, frequent warnings can be issued via television and radio. Websites also provide information on every storm around the globe.

↓ Scientists use planes like the one shown below to journey into the eye of the hurricane. The plane's probe, which is located in front of the nose, gives instant information on the pressure and humidity inside the hurricane, thereby enabling scientists to calculate its strength.

# FACT FILE

### The cyclones that hit Bangladesh

Bangladesh has been the victim of many cyclones, which cause flooding of the Ganges delta. In 1970, a tropical cyclone claimed 500,000 lives there. Thousands died in 1985 when a massive wall of water swept over the mudflats where people lived and farmed the land. In April 1991, a devastating cyclone raced into the Bay of Bengal at 143 mph, and waves nearly 23 feet high flooded many communities on the coast. It is thought that 250,000 people may have been killed, some of them on fishing boats and others in flimsy houses made of mud and straw. This was the worst cyclone to hit Bangladesh in the 20th century, with stronger winds than the 1970 storm. Warnings were given, but many people did not have radios or television so they did not hear them. About 10 million people were left homeless and millions more people may have died from starvation and diseases such as cholera.

### Tropical storms in history

**1737**—Cyclone storm surge killed 300,000 people in the Calcutta area of India.

**1899**— 300 people killed in Bathurst, Queensland, Australia, by a 49 ft storm surge, formed as a result of cyclone winds.

**1900**—A hurricane and storm surge hit Galveston, Texas, causing about 6,000 deaths.

**1945**—2,000 people killed by a typhoon in Japan—just 42 days after the devastation of Hiroshima by a nuclear bomb.

## RECENT TROPICAL STORMS

### 1999

**Bangladesh**—107 people died in a June cyclone that swept in from the Bay of Bengal. The death toll was relatively low because of improvements in cyclone shelters and evacuation procedures.

**U.S.**—Three million Americans were affected by Hurricane Floyd, which packed 155 mph winds.

**India**—In November, Orissa state was torn apart by a supercyclone which killed over 10,000 people.

### 2000

**Madagascar**—In spring, cyclones Eline, Gloria, and Hudar lashed at Madagascar. Leaving 100,000 homeless, the cyclones went on to devastate Mozambique.

**Central America**—Hurricanes Keith and Gordon swept across several Central American states in September, causing scores of fatalities.

### 2001

**Philippines**—In July, the Philippines were battered by typhoons Durian and Utor, which both went on to drench Taiwan and southern China.

**U.S.**—Tropical storm Allison soaked the southern U.S. coast in June, causing $4.8 billion worth of damage.

### 2002

**South Korea**—In September, Typhoon Rusa, the most powerful typhoon to hit South Korea in 40 years, left at least 100 people dead and scores many more missing in flash floods and landslides.

**Mexico**—Hurricane Kenna made landfall near San Blas with winds of 150 mph. Only 5% of homes in San Blas remained intact after the hurricane.

### 2003

**U.S.**—Hurricane Isabel came ashore in September, causing 38 fatalities in North Carolina. It was the first Atlantic hurricane to reach category five since Hurricane Mitch in 1998.

**Fiji**—In January, tropical cyclone Ami battered Fiji and surrounding islands with winds of 115 mph, causing 15 deaths, substantial flooding, and millions of dollars worth of damage.

### Tornado terrors

The United States has more than 850 tornadoes every year. Most tornadoes occur between April and October. The most disastrous, in terms of lives lost, was in the midwestern states in 1925, when 689 people were killed. But others have had devastating consequences, too. In April 1979, a tornado struck the city of Wichita Falls in Texas. By the time it had passed, the city looked as though it had been bombed: 20,000 people were left homeless and 46 were killed. Sometimes, several tornadoes start at once. In 1974, 148 tornadoes killed 315 people in 13 states over a period of two days. In May 1999, devastating tornadoes tore through Oklahoma and Kansas, killing around 50 people. The largest cut a path about one mile wide as it swept across Oklahoma City, and 76 tornadoes occurred in total. In November 2002, 75 tornadoes touched down in one day, causing damage in 13 states.

# GLOSSARY

**air pressure**—the weight of the air in the lower layers of the atmosphere pressing down on the earth. This is always changing as air moves around. Warm air rises and expands. It becomes thinner and lighter, so it does not press down on the earth so hard, creating an area of low pressure. Low pressure areas, or "lows," bring cloudy, rainy weather because the air high up cools, and moisture condenses into clouds. As the cool air descends again, it becomes heavier, so it is at high pressure. The air warms up as it sinks, and clouds disappear. So, a "high" often brings dry, clear weather.

**atmosphere**—the envelope of gases that surround the earth. The atmosphere protects us from the sun and also provides us with the oxygen we need to breathe.

**Beaufort Scale**—a scale of wind speeds that is based on things that can be easily seen, such as smoke, trees, and damage caused. The Beaufort numbers range between 0 and 12, grading winds from calm to hurricane force. The scale was devised by Admiral Sir Francis Beaufort and is the official method of describing wind speeds.

**condense**—to turn from water vapor into tiny drops of water. You can see this happening to steam from a bath when it hits a cold surface such as a wall or window.

**cyclone**—the name for tropical storms when they occur in the Indian Ocean.

**evacuate**—to remove people from a place that is considered dangerous.

**eye**—the calm, cloudless center of a hurricane, cyclone, or typhoon.

**front**—the boundary between a mass of warm, moist air and a mass of cold, dry air.

**global warming**—the heating up of the earth by a build-up of carbon dioxide and other "greenhouse" gases in the atmosphere. Heat cannot escape back into space and so the Greenhouse Effect is increased. This may cause the planet to warm up, possibly to a dangerous degree.

**hemisphere**—half a sphere. The equator divides the earth into the Northern Hemisphere and the Southern Hemisphere.

**meteorologist**—someone who studies information about weather conditions and prepares a weather forecast.

**monsoon**—the rainy season in India and Southeast Asia. In the summer, moist wind blows in from the Indian Ocean, bringing heavy rain. In the fall, cool, dry winds blow out from the land, bringing dry weather.

**satellite**—a small object moving around a larger one, such as the moon moving around earth. Weather satellites are manmade devices that orbit the earth and send back weather information.

**storm surge**—massive waves that build up out at sea as a tropical storm blows in.

**temperate**—describes a climate that has four seasons—spring, summer, fall, and winter.

**thermal current**—a current of air that is rising because it has been heated.

**tornado**—the name for violent tropical storms that occur overland, mainly in the U.S.

**tropics**—the part of the earth between the Tropic of Cancer and the Tropic of Capricorn. The weather is hottest at the equator.

**typhoon**—the name for tropical storms when they occur in the Far East.

# INDEX

## Photocredits

**Abbreviations: l-left, r-right, b-bottom, t-top, c-center, m-middle**